STEM JOBS IN
Fashion and Beauty

Carla Mooney

Rourke
Educational Media

rourkeeducationalmedia.com

Before Reading:

Building Academic Vocabulary and Background Knowledge

Before reading a book, it is important to tap into what your child or students already know about the topic. This will help them develop their vocabulary, increase their reading comprehension, and make connections across the curriculum.

1. Look at the cover of the book. What will this book be about?
2. What do you already know about the topic?
3. Let's study the Table of Contents. What will you learn about in the book's chapters?
4. What would you like to learn about this topic? Do you think you might learn about it from this book? Why or why not?
5. Use a reading journal to write about your knowledge of this topic. Record what you already know about the topic and what you hope to learn about the topic.
6. Read the book.
7. In your reading journal, record what you learned about the topic and your response to the book.
8. After reading the book complete the activities below.

Content Area Vocabulary

Read the list. What do these words mean?

analysts
consumers
focus groups
formulations
innovation
markup
patent
photosensitivity
position
production
profit margin
sustainable
synthetic
trends

After Reading:

Comprehension and Extension Activity

After reading the book, work on the following questions with your child or students in order to check their level of reading comprehension and content mastery.

1. Describe the role of STEM in the fashion and beauty industry. (Summarize)
2. Why might some companies have stopped testing their products' safety on animals? (Infer)
3. How is it helpful to have a variety of shampoos to choose from at a drug store? (Text to self connection)
4. How do market researchers use data? (Summarize)
5. Describe how a product's placement in a store makes people more likely to buy it. (Visualize)

Extension Activity

Choose one product you use regularly, such as shampoo, lip balm, or moisturizer. Get a sample of a variety of brands and compare each product on a number of factors, such as price, packaging, smell, effectiveness, and any other qualities you consider important. Analyze your data and offer your recommendation for the best product.

Table of Contents

What Is STEM?

Would you like to work as a fashion designer using a computer program to design a dress for a Paris fashion show? How about a chemist testing different **formulations** for a new face cream? Or maybe a web designer creating an online site where customers can view and purchase a company's clothing line?

These people all have great jobs in fashion and beauty. But they have something else in common, too. All their jobs require a STEM education. STEM is a shortcut for talking about science, technology, engineering, and mathematics.

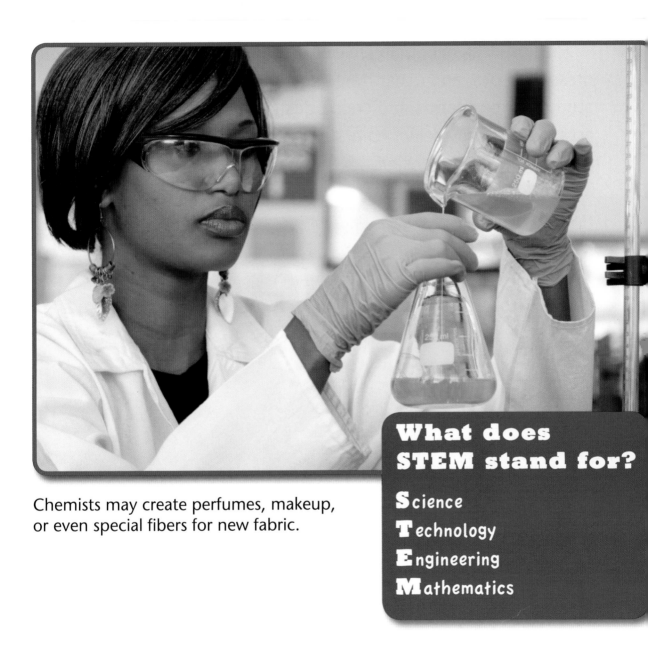

Chemists may create perfumes, makeup, or even special fibers for new fabric.

All industries need people with STEM skills to build and develop the next great thing. A strong STEM education will prepare you for unique careers in the exciting world of fashion and beauty. What great STEM jobs are waiting for you?

Hi-Tech Fashion Design

Fashion designers help create the billions of shirts, suits, dresses, shoes, and other items sold every year. Designers study fashion **trends** and create designs of new clothing and accessories. They select colors and fabrics. They oversee the **production** of the design.

In the fashion industry, a new collection is created with more than fabric and thread. Fashion designers rely on hi-tech computers and software to design clothing and construct patterns. Using computer-aided design (CAD) programs, designers experiment with ideas. CAD programs show the designer what the finished garment will look like.

Designers construct patterns for their clothing so that the items can be mass-produced.

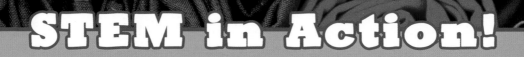

STEM in Action!

When proposing a new design to the sales team, a fashion designer needs to understand the cost of creating the garment. He or she will use mathematics to calculate the garment's cost.

Let's say that the materials to make a new skirt design are as follows:

Material	Units Used	Cost per Unit
Silk fabric	3 yards	$3 per yard
Lining	3 yards	$2 per yard
Thread	12 yards	$0.50 per yard
Labor (cutting & sewing)	1 hour	$15 per hour

How much will the skirt cost to make?

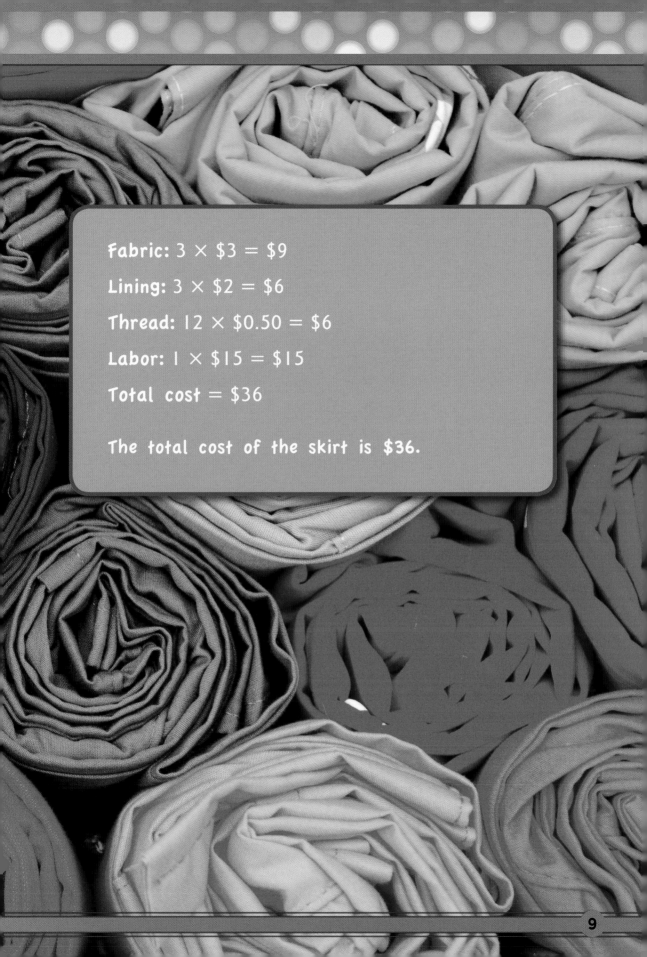

Fabric: 3 × $3 = $9

Lining: 3 × $2 = $6

Thread: 12 × $0.50 = $6

Labor: 1 × $15 = $15

Total cost = $36

The total cost of the skirt is $36.

Designers use CAD software to design individual pieces of clothing or entire collections. They use the software to draw garments, add color, create woven textures, drape fabric over models, and adjust sizing. Using computer technology, fashion designers can easily create multiple samples and variations. When finalized, CAD designs can be used in sales presentations.

STEM Spotlight: Eco-Friendly Clothing

Some fashion designers are using science to develop new fabrics and designs. British fashion designer Stella McCartney was one of the first designers to support **sustainable** fashion.

Today, many fashion houses are creating eco-friendly clothing. They use recycled materials and organically grown materials to create new garments.

Developing New Products

Thousands of perfumes, lotions, cosmetics, and hair products line store shelves. Who creates all of these products? This is the job of cosmetic scientists who work in the beauty industry. They invent and improve hair, skin care, and makeup products.

Cosmetic scientists work in labs where they develop recipes for new products. They learn the formulas of existing products so that they can understand how each product works. Then they use that knowledge to develop new and improved formulas. They create beauty products that make people feel better, younger, and more confident.

To create a new product, cosmetic scientists mix and measure ingredients. They test each recipe and measure how effective it is. Scientists who develop hair products test hair samples to see which formula creates the most shine or best improves hair strength. Sometimes, a cosmetic scientist will file a **patent** for a new product formula.

Real STEM Job: *L'Oréal Scientist*

L'Oréal is a leading cosmetics and beauty company. L'Oréal has many scientists that work in research and **innovation**. They study current hair, skin, and beauty products. They experiment with new formulas, ingredients, and processing techniques to create the next new line of beauty products.

This job requires a science background. Cosmetic scientists have studied chemistry, biochemistry, physiology, and other related science fields. They explore and innovate with different materials and methods. They know how to analyze, organize, and present data from their experiments. It is a great job for people who like to mix and invent things.

A cosmetic scientist may work individually or as part of a team. Some become leaders who direct groups of scientists.

Cosmetic scientists working on skin care study the effects of natural and **synthetic** compounds on the skin. They test a compound to see how it affects skin aging. One of the most famous biotechnology products used in skin care is Botox. Botox is a protein made by a bacteria. It paralyzes nerve cells, which reduces wrinkles.

Botox is injected into the skin and may be effective at reducing wrinkles for up to four months.

STEM in Action!

A formula is like a recipe. Ingredients are mixed together in specific amounts to create the final product. For example, a test recipe for a raspberry sugar scrub may call for the following ingredients:

4 ounces of fresh raspberries
1 cup sugar
1 tablespoon olive oil
1 drop of almond extract
1 drop of peppermint extract

Test the scrub. How does it feel on your skin? Does it need more scrubbing power or does it feel too rough? How do you like the smell?

Adjust the recipe to improve the scrub and test it again. Keep testing until you find a scrub that works just right for you.

Product Safety

Beauty products contain chemicals and other ingredients that could cause side effects when used. Companies that make beauty products want to make sure that their products are safe for **consumers**. Before the products are sold, scientists conduct safety tests.

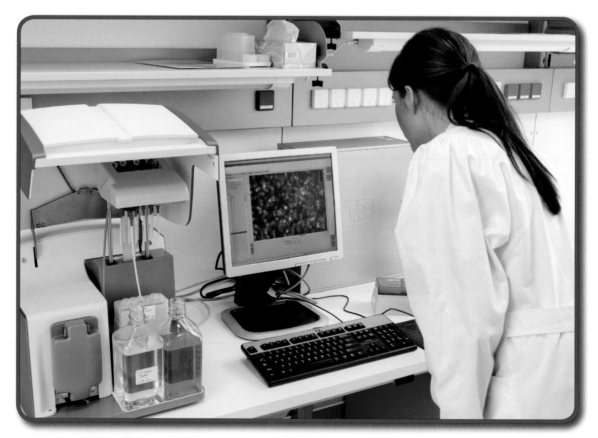

Chemists may analyze products to figure out what compound may be causing a bad reaction.

STEM Spotlight: Cosmetic Safety

In the United States, the Federal Government does not review or regulate what goes into cosmetic products. Some states have laws that govern cosmetics. But for the most part, cosmetic companies are responsible for making sure their products are safe. Fortunately, many companies agree that product safety is a top priority! They have agreed not to use toxic chemicals in their products.

Product safety scientists test products to see if they cause skin irritation. They test to see if the products cause **photosensitivity.** Products such as mascaras and eye creams must be tested to see if they cause eye irritation. Safety scientists also test to see if products can be absorbed through the skin. Depending on the purpose of the product, this could be a good or bad thing!

sensitive

At one time, beauty products were frequently tested on animals. Today, scientists have developed alternative ways to test many products safely without using animals. For example, they may test their products on cells in a petri dish, instead of a live animal. This has made it possible for consumers to buy safe products that have not harmed animals.

STEM Fast Fact: L'Oréal has developed an artificial human skin that can be used to test if new products cause irritation.

STEM in Action!

Scientists analyze and present data from safety testing. A skin cream is tested on 100 volunteers. Ninety-five volunteers report no side effects from the cream. Two volunteers report an itchy rash after applying the product. Three volunteers report red welts after applying the cream. The product safety scientists decide to test the cream on 100 additional volunteers. This time, only one volunteer reports a rash from the cream. How will the scientists present all of the test data to the company?

Total volunteers in testing:
$$100 + 100 = 200$$
Volunteers who reported a skin reaction:
$$2 + 3 + 1 = 6$$

The scientist reports that 6 volunteers out of 200, or 3 percent, experienced a skin reaction. The company may decide this percentage is too high. Then the product will be sent back to cosmetic scientists to improve it.

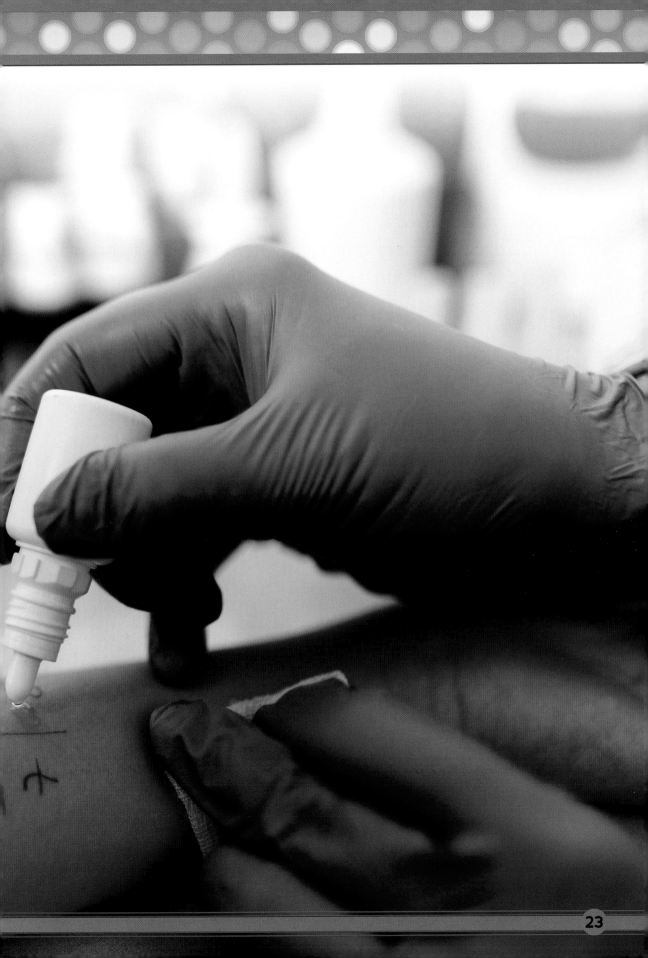

Market Research

How do companies know what products customers want to buy? Market research **analysts** study customer behavior. They investigate what drives a person to buy a product. Some analysts may work directly for a fashion or beauty company. Others may work for a firm that is hired by the company.

Real STEM Job:
Market Research Account Analyst at the NPD Group

The NPD Group works with some of the most well-known and exciting fashion companies in the world. Account analysts there study data for clients. They look at what people are buying, where they are buying it, and how much they are paying. They use statistics to identify trends in fashion, footwear, accessories, and beauty.

This job requires strong analytical skills. However, in order to understand the information they are looking at, market analysts also need to understand the fashion and beauty industry. NPD Group analysts study data, figure out what it means, and share their findings with clients.

Market research analysts collect a lot of data. They interview people in **focus groups** about new products. They collect data about consumer buying habits. They conduct surveys about shopping habits. They track sales in different types of stores.

Market analysts look at people's responses to focus group questions to understand how people feel about their product.

Market researchers use statistics to understand the data they collect. Armed with this data, researchers know what their customers want. They can create ads that better appeal to the kinds of people buying their product. Or, they can change the price of the product so that people are more likely to buy it. Market research analysts use customer data to help companies decide what new products their customers will buy.

delivered solid results in a challenging market

Projected sales of main products in 2013

Distribution of market share among the major industry players

18 14 45 89 29 86 95 14 155 121 147 184 172 210 259 124 280 295 320

STEM in Action!

A market research analyst conducts several focus groups to find out how people choose what new athletic shoe to buy. There are a total of 100 people in the focus group. When asked what the most important factor in their shoe buying decision is, the participants reported:

Style: 50 people
Price: 35 people
Brand: 10 people
Availability: 5 people

How will the analyst present this information to the company? He or she may choose to create a graph or chart.

How would you improve this survey? Would it be helpful to know the age of the participants? How about the kinds of sports they play? Put together your own list of questions. Then ask your friends, family, and classmates to complete your survey. Make a chart to share your new data.

Factors in Shoe Buying!

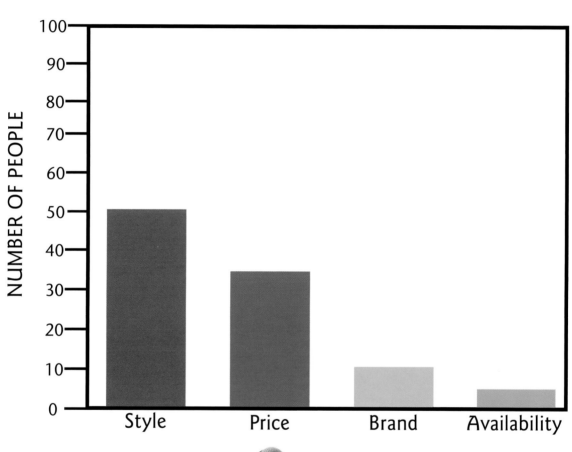

NUMBER OF PEOPLE

100
90
80
70
60
50
40
30
20
10
0

Style   Price   Brand   Availability

Merchandising

Who decides what shirts a store is going to sell next spring? Who decides the price of a new eye shadow line? The fashion and beauty industry hires merchandisers to work with products and set sales goals for stores.

A merchandiser is always thinking about the best way to **position** a product so that it will sell. When merchandisers position a product, they think about how their product will get the most sales. They decide what stores should sell their product and how much it should cost. They think about how a customer sees their product in a store. They work with designers to create appealing product packaging. They help stores place products in appealing displays.

An attractive display in a store will draw more buyers.

Setting the price for a product is an important part of a merchandiser's job. A merchandiser sets a product's price, its **markup** over cost, and how much profit it will make. He or she also sets sales goals and budgets.

Once a product is in a store, a merchandiser analyzes sales. Sales numbers show what is selling and what is not. The merchandiser makes sure that a store has the right amount and mix of stock. He or she also studies how their product is selling compared to other similar products.

Sales data is essential in deciding which products are successful.

STEM in Action!

A product's **profit margin** is the difference between its expenses, or how much it costs to make, and its revenue, or sales price. Profit can be expressed in the following formula:

Profit = Revenue - Expenses

A merchandiser will develop price points for a new product. If a perfume costs $40 to make and the company wants to make a $10 profit, what should be the perfume's price?

Profit = Revenue – Expenses
$10 = Revenue - $40

Balance the equation.

$10 + $40 = Revenue
$50 = Revenue

The merchandiser will make the perfume's price $50.

Real STEM Job:
Product Merchandiser at Nordstrom

Nordstrom uses a team of merchandisers to help the company create and sell cutting-edge fashion. Each day, product merchandisers gather and analyze sales data. They research the market and competitors. Then, they develop merchandise plans based on their knowledge and analysis.

This job requires strong math and analytical skills. Merchandisers calculate and analyze gross margins, markups, and profitability. They are skilled at analyzing and processing complex data. They also use a variety of computer programs to gather and organize data. Merchandisers then share the results of their analysis with others.

At a store level, a merchandiser may choose to present products in a new display or offer discounts to make items sell better.

Web Development

Almost every company today has a website. Customers visit a company's website to learn more about products, find store locations, and buy products online. Creating a website that is creative, attractive, and useful to customers is the job of web developers.

Web developers create specialized, eye-catching websites for the fashion and beauty industry. Web developers use color, images, layouts, photos, and fonts to create stylish and chic websites for the fashion and beauty industry.

Because every company is different, web developers work with each company to create a site that reflects the company's needs. Some companies want to sell their products online. Others want to show new product information. Or they may want to create a community where their customers can share their ideas. Web developers learn the company's goals and then create a website.

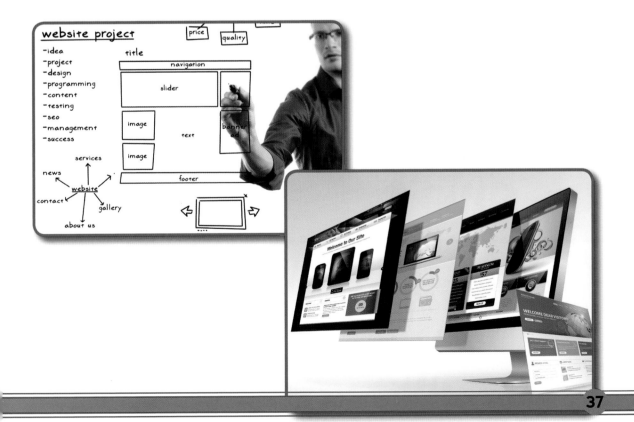

```
tring
if(parameters.contains("
    hql += "  and p.name = :n
}

if(parameters.contains("
    hql += "  and p.age =
}

TypedQuery<Person> qu

if(parameters.contai
    query.setParameter
```

STEM in Action!

Web developers know how to use HTML coding to build websites. HTML stands for HyperText Markup Language. It is the language used to create web pages that can be displayed in a web browser. HTML uses tags to mark blocks of text on a page. One of the most common HTML tags used is the <strong> or bold tag. It is used to mark text that should be bolded. For example, `<strong>this is bold text</strong>`.

How would a developer code the following sentence to make the words "New Products" bold?

Beauty company launches line of New Products on Thursday.

it would be coded as follows:

```
Beauty company launches line of
<strong>New Products</strong> on
Thursday.
```

The code would appear on the website as:

Beauty company launches line of **New Products** on Thursday.

Real STEM Job:
BCBG Web Production Artist

At BCBG, web production artists work with designers on email campaigns, banners, landing pages, and other parts of the company's website. Working with other team members, they design company websites from the initial idea to a working site. They use computer and Web skills to build, maintain, and troubleshoot the sites.

This job requires strong computer skills. Web production artists know about web design and coding. They are skilled at web programming using HTML and CSS. They know how to use computer programs such as Adobe Photoshop, Flash FTP, and Microsoft Project. For someone who enjoys both computers and fashion, this job may be the perfect combination!

STEM Careers

Some of the most exciting careers in fashion and beauty are in STEM fields. Jobs in design, product development, and merchandising are just some examples of fashion and beauty careers that use STEM skills every day. The skills you learn from STEM subjects can be a great foundation for almost any career you choose!

STEM Job Fact Sheets

Fashion Designer

Important Skills: Critical Thinking, Mathematics, Computer-Aided Design

Important Knowledge: Fashion, Textiles, Fabrics, Fashion Merchandising

College Major: Art, Fashion Design, Textile Design

Median Salary: $64,530

Chemist and Materials Scientist

Important Skills: Problem-Solving, Critical Thinking, Computer Skills, Mathematics

Important Knowledge: Chemistry, Mathematics, and related science fields

College Major: Chemistry or related science degree

Median Salary: $69,970

Product Safety Scientist

Important Skills: Problem-Solving, Critical Thinking, Computer Skills, Mathematics

Important Knowledge: Chemistry, Toxicology, Anatomy, and related science fields

College Major: Chemistry or related science degree

Median Salary: $69,970*

*Data provided is for materials scientist

Market Research Analyst

Important Skills: Mathematics, Analytical Skills, Writing Skills

Important Knowledge: Mathematics, Fashion and Beauty Industry, Statistics, Computer Science

College Major: Market Research, Mathematics, or Statistics

Median Salary: $60,570

Merchandiser

Important Skills: Mathematics, Analytical Thinking, Retail, Marketing, Computer Skills

Important Knowledge: Fashion and Beauty, Marketing, Mathematics

College Major: Fashion Merchandising or Marketing

Median Salary: $80,831

Web Developer

Important Skills: Computer and Web Skills, Design, Creativity

Important Knowledge: HTML, JavaScript, Adobe Photoshop, Flash, CSS, and related programs

College Major: Computer Science or related field

Median Salary: $62,500

Glossary

analysts (AN-uh-lists): people who examine data and draw conclusions from it

consumers (kuhn-SOO-murs): people who buy and use products and services

focus groups (FOH-kuhss groops): a group of people who are asked about their thoughts and perceptions about a product or service

formulations (for-myuh-LAY-shunz): the recipe or instructions used to make a product

innovation (in-uh-VAY-shuhn): a new idea or invention

markup (MARK-up): the difference between the cost of a product and its selling price

patent (PAT-uhnt): a legal document giving the inventor of an item the sole rights to manufacture or sell it

photosensitivity (foh-toh-sen-si-TIV-i-tee): abnormal sensitivity to sunlight

position (puh-ZISH-uhn): placing a product in the market compared to similar products

production (pruh-DUHK-shuhn): the process of making something

profit margin (PROF-it MAR-juhn): the cost of making and selling a product subtracted from the selling price

sustainable (suh-STEY-nuh-buhl): seeks to reduce harm to the environment

synthetic (sin-THET-ik): something that is manufactured or artificial and not found in nature

trends (TRENDZ): the latest popular fashions

Index

Show What You Know

1. What does STEM stand for?
2. What STEM skills are used in fashion design?
3. How is math used in fashion merchandising?
4. What type of science jobs can be found in a beauty company?
5. What characteristics does a successful web developer need to have?

Websites to Visit

http://forgirlsinscience.org

http://stemcareer.com/

http://www.coolsciencecareers.rice.edu/

About the Author

Carla Mooney has written many books for children and young adults. She lives in Pennsylvania with her husband and three children. She enjoys learning about how science can be used in a variety of areas and careers.

Meet The Author!
www.meetREMauthors.com

PHOTO CREDITS: Cover © Roob, AlexRaths, Ben Blankenburg, mumininan; Title Page © wavebreakmedia; page 4 © Image Source; page 5 © PhotoSky; page 6 © Kzenon; page 7 © Diego Cervo; page 8 © Operation Shooting; page 10 © Blend_Images; page 11 © Gemanacom, Featureflash; page 12 © Sergey Novikov; page 13 © photomim; page 14 © Pressmaster; page 15 © Alexander Raths, Zoltan Kiraly; page 16 © Robert Kneschke; page 17 © kubais, iofoto; page 18 © Lisa S.; page 19, 37 © Pure Solution; page 20 © dndavis, natasha58; page 21 © lupulluss; page 22 © gorillaimages; page 24 © OPOLJA; page 25 © Andreyuu, Kheng Guan Toh; page 26 © Pixooz; page 27 © Andriy Popov, Sergey Nivens; page 29, 37 © ronstik; page 30 © Olesya Feketa; page 31 © Oleg Golovnev; page 32 © Tagstock Japan; page 33 © jaywarren79; page 35 © DmitriMaruta; page 36 © Northfoto; page 38 © isak55; page 41 © CEFutcher; page 42 © Andresr; page 43 © catwalker

Edited by: Jill Sherman

Cover design by: Renee Brady
Interior design by: Rhea Magaro

Library of Congress PCN Data

STEM Jobs in Fashion and Beauty / Carla Mooney
(STEM Jobs You'll Love)
 ISBN 978-1-62717-700-9 (hard cover)
 ISBN 978-1-62717-822-8 (soft cover)
 ISBN 978-1-62717-936-2 (e-Book)
Library of Congress Control Number: 2014935493

Printed in the United States of America, North Mankato, Minnesota

Also Available as:
ROURKE'S
e-Books